Gallery Books
Editor: Peter Fallon

HAICÉAD

Michael Hartnett

HAICÉAD

Gallery Books

Haicéad
is first published
simultaneously in paperback
and in a clothbound edition
on 11 November 1993.

The Gallery Press
Loughcrew
Oldcastle
County Meath
Ireland

ISBN 1 85235 108 X (*paperback*)
     1 85235 109 8 (*clothbound*)

The Gallery Press receives financial assistance from An Chomhairle
Ealaíon / The Arts Council, Ireland.

Contents

for Máire Ní Cheallacháin

Preface

The year and place of Pádraigín Haicéad's birth is not known. O'Heyne, in his *Irish Dominicans of the Seventeenth Century*, says he belonged to the Cashel (Co. Tipperary) community and the date 1622 occurs in the title of one of his early poems. Other dated titles give indications of his whereabouts at different times: 1628, London; 1630, Louvain; 1632, Morlaix (France). A poem to the harper Eoghan Ó Eachach has the heading *Déis gur shinn Eoghan mfailte go heirinn 1613* — (After Eoghan played my welcome to Ireland) — with the confusing '1613' as a probable mistranscription of '1633'. O'Heyne states he was prior of his convent (Cashel) and was made chief Preacher in 1644. He was in Clonmel in 1647 and in Louvain once more in 1651, where he died three years later.

The above paragraph is but a *précis* of a life full of rage and patriotism; of the life of a poet-priest capable of delicate conceits, of puns and tenderness, of savage poems inciting to war and carnage; of the life of a Gaelic poet who could lament in moving language the deaths of his adopted chieftains; of the life of a poet-priest who left no prayers of repentance and whose last verses brought curses down on his fellow clergymen. When Rinuccini, the Papal Nuncio, broke with the Kilkenny Confederation in 1646, Haicéad was soon, in Clonmel, 'fostering contention' among the soldiers. *Airnéis*, to him, also meant 'cattle'; add the Irish diminutive '-ín' and you have *Caitlín*; *beannacht* becomes bean nocht — a salutation becomes a naked woman! He could invoke 'the God of Grace' to help Ireland and in the next verse say:

> May the edge of the sharp spears by hate honed,
> wielded by our chivalry — our youths as their
>   support —
> deal deadly blows, piercing to the bone,
> and slashing and tearing, annihilate the foe!

And he could write a lovely, if conventional, 'court of love' effusion to Mary Tobin and, shortly afterwards, on hearing of her death, write a *real* and tender poem. His laments for two of the Butlers, Éamon (Poem 29) and Richard (Poem 43) are written in conventional elegiac metre (brilliantly handled, in the original); but while in Poem 29 the *caoineadh* is in the old mode, with all its genealogical and topographical trappings, Poem 43 abandons almost all of these and treats its subject, not so much as a distinguished corpse of long pedigree, but as a man of action.

Having backed Rinuccini, Rome, and the Dominican Order for most of his life, he hears, in his last days, that the Irish clergy has been forbidden by its bishops to write poetry in the Irish language. He does not obey this edict. I have described him as a 'poet-priest' and 'priest-poet', but he belonged to an order older than any in Christendom and in his last poem (49) rejoins it triumphantly.

In his last two years he is querulous and bitter; he is passed over for promotion, he argues over money, he bickers with his superiors; his proposal to write a book (*two* proposed books are known of — one genealogical, the other treating of how the anti-Catholic group failed at the Confederation of Kilkenny — this may have been the one objected to) is not acceptable: indeed, he is threatened with confinement if he dares to publish it. At last his superiors decide that he is going out of his mind. In a letter dated 19 December 1654, De Marinis, the Italian head of the Dominican Order, writing to the Provincial of the Low Countries, says he has recieved his letter of 20 November which contained a report of Haicéad's complaint against the head of the Dominican house in Louvain. He (De Marinis) says, 'God Himself, however, has closed the case: He has sent for Haicéad to appear before His own judgement seat'.

Note on the Translations

I have tried here to show the variety of Haicéad's metres and the variety of his themes. I have not, of course, caught the beauty of his Irish. Some of the close-lipped Irish-speaking writers of today do not approve of translations from the language: it is as if they did do not wish to share poets they do not read themselves. A translation is, at best, an illuminating footnote to the original; and I hope that readers of this book will not be led away from but towards the real Haicéad.

Acknowledgements

This book would not have come about if it were not for the initial suggestion made to me by Fr. Paul Murray, Dominican of Tallaght, and for his kindness in providing me with much material; if it were not for Jean Barry who typed the manuscript; for Peter Fallon for his patience; but, especially, if it were not for Máire Ní Cheallacháin, author of *Filíocht Phádraigín Haicéad* (An Clóchomhar 1962), who provided me with a literal translation and who, over the last two years, has followed the progress of this work comma by comma. She has suggested many amendments to these translations, most of which I adopted. I dedicate this book to her.

1

Though I am just a wisp of straw and not a besom —
and not Cearúl — that noble, handsome creature —
I'd sooner have his place in your affections
than control the whole of Cruachain's taxes.

Take heed — although he's absent long on trips —
don't ignore my love in such hardships;
for it's commonly said, my girl, whose tight curls thickly fall,
it's better to be mangy than have no hair at all.

2

In sleep, O people, do you think I'll long survive
her magic chant which takes away my soul alive,
this creature with her breasts as white as fleece
who fetters up my body with disease?

She unlooses yellow hair down to the grass,
countless branching ringlets in a mass:
with my contorted face all that I can see
is the wild blood blazing in her cheeks.

This witch with primal magic handed down
has driven hundreds underneath the ground
and by this magic, we, eternally oppressed
and ever wrangling, are beguiled and wretched.

I call on Michael, the steward of the king:
for she, with her cunning and her sensual skill,

has reduced me to this craven state,
utterly exhausted and enslaved.

3

A sad and bitter story about us goes around —
it makes me blind to all things and deaf to every sound —
that Deirdre of the unrevealing eyes has said
that we must separate, for she intends to wed.

And thus I fear I'll not survive a month, but fade —
and my good looks are gone, so total is the change;
for my shrieks the birds of Ireland soar into the air,
my tears flow fast like undercurrents in a lake.

Alas, it is no fault of the slender noble svelte
sweet silvertongued whitetoothed girl
to quietly take advice from her astuter friends
and be harnessed to a freeborn mate who'd treat her well
    when wed.

I think myself if anyone compared the two of us,
and she went with me, Oh God, they'd think it hard luck:
she, handsome graceful wise with twisting intricate hair,
a white-as-chalk and stately smoothflanked maid,

and I, poor wretch, without a daring deed to tell
no realm falls to my lot and I've lost all my wealth
and my body is so thin I'd go easily through a net —
and Ó Néill is of a noble clan — pity they're all dead!

4

To Mary Tobin

Like the daisy when first it sees the sun
and its interlocking petals loosen all at once
or in the evening at the first cloud's cover
when its seedhead by a leaf is sheltered over:

so I, when this sweet distinguished friend —
Mary Tobin, breath of air, that storms the fighting men;
my true-voiced love who moves with gentle ease —
when I'm with her my heart pours out a gentle peace;

and if she leaves, my virgin of the perfect breasts,
my heart does not allow me sensibly to rest
but moves like the white eternal daisy of the field
and drowns me in the clamour of a bitter grief.

Though fruits do not seed on the crown of her head
yet the crocus comes forth, where there is no earth
and around goes a plait, glittering, in the form
of a birdflock tired from a winter storm.

A stroke from a sharpened quill is not more slim
than her eyebrows black as the beetle's wing
above her eyes — two spheres of liquid grey —
the archetypal rose is in the whiteness of her face;

her fine and smooth and well-proportioned nose,
her gentle lips that well-shaped teeth enclose —
lovely her holy hand fashioning needlework,
lovely her throat's hue beside which lime seems dull.

Entrancing music in our land gives not more peaceful sound,
the expert harpist's air has no more eloquence
than the smallest saying of her sweet mouth
that lifts the fog that clouds up all my sense.

Many young men come, all of Norman-Irish seed,
unmanned in the embers of their aching need:
instead of these, to choose such a wretch as I?
No better than death my life: no richer she that I die.

5

After hearing of Mary's death

My quiet pleasant man: disquieting's the news you tell —
away with their cries who in dirges hid my angel!
They are wrong: it is far better to be dumb
than be party to a noise that makes their voices venom-full.

Take its sound away: I do not wish to know or hear
this terrible and ugly clamorous grief:
though all think my girl is left in the ground to die
death has not conquered her image in my mind.

Her beauty stays intact: not a jot is changed;
she is known to be warm, affectionate,
devout and honest, pure and wise,
pleasant, lovely, noble, young and kind.

No sadder saying than to say she died before her noon
in the promise of her flower, in the Spring of her youth,

my small pure lamb without disease, deceit,
no jeering, no cajolery, impurity or tears;

(and unless a tomb was full of the many now alive
it's hardly worth mentioning the slaughter of their kind)
it is a heavy fine that only gold accepts
from people who pay tin as their usual tax.

And I've become a fable, a phantom, a dream;
pity me, unpitied: I've been willingly deceived
but now hard fact torments me, exhausts me to ruin:
I know that when you spoke of her you spoke truth.

Death's new strength, which has stopped my drinking-bouts,
makes me live in a lonely place, pleasure puts to rout,
makes my face withered and my strength weak,
will yet cause rain to fall in these cold Irish fields.

Trouble, downfall, loss, sorrow without relief
make me hate all trades, make me drunk with grief
and pour wild streams of tears out of caves of bone
so that my life's threads suspended float.

For my departed love I'd be a bad exchange
if just this once I went to death instead —
but I have received the grace to forever suffer pain
in the stinging fire of hurt among the living dead.

As every heron flies with its own kind
so Mary sailed with speed to her angel's side:
my blackbird, take my blessing and embrace your Paradise —
for my virgin girl, this is not death — but life.

6

*To Captain Carey's Company, from London
to Canterbury, 1628*

My life on the boys so strong when times were hard
in England of the Kings or in the cold French lands,
who when the fight was on, reduced with active steel
the ravenous dour aliens to a putrid rubbish heap!

The lively, formidable, funloving fighting men
who, fierce and young and manly, hated treachery so well;
and it's hard to establish that Guaire banished greed
better than they as they daily provide for the clan and their
    needs.

Since I must now be always away and in their debt
(woe to the staunchest recruit who stands in their path!)
Christ of his charity, care for that graceful muster of men
and from me let them have an orphan's grateful small blessing
    as well.

7

In Louvain, 1630

Though to chosen chieftains I did give my hand —
men worthy of affection in my ancestral land —
I'm considered in this country to be a mere lad
with *'as er se'** the only knowledge that I have.

---

*So things are.

It is of no importance: I will have my day
and without fear of any man, this I here proclaim:
if the people who insult me are for wisdom known
then the noblemen in Ireland are merely dolts.

8

In Louvain, 1630

O gentle company far off on Ireland's plain
let us speak of learning and put grief away;
let us get down to business as all men must:
on behalf of Ireland let us drink a toast.

But with this clique here to whom I pledged my heart —
who never offered me a hint of one kind act,
woe to the poor insignificant friendless man
who burned for them his pallet and harp!

9

To Cearúl Óg Ó Dálaigh, 1630

Of a certain Cearúl in Ireland
a great account I heard
for noble ways of wisdom,
for poetic sparkling words;

for alacrity, dexterity,
fluency, lovableness,

for tricks of speech and music,
for knowing many spells;

the Cearúl I heard mentioned
was beloved of the girls —
find his like in the Low Countries
among kings or churls!

It's no good telling me now
that this tale is unadorned
when the saying really goes
'far-off cows have long horns'.

Unless it was another
of whom the story ran,
it's no mistake to say of him:
'Cearúl Ó Dálaigh's the man!'

10

Cearúl's Answer

I'm not the man you heard of
in your land of fighting-men,
I'm not a craftsman in that class;
but I *do* exist — unlike him.

I, no smith, no poet,
no juggler, fuller am,
no weaver on reeded looms;
I'm an unknown man.

I am not abroad or home
such a mythical being;
I don't and won't exist for *you:*
Hacket, stop your idle speech.

If you're the one described
don't pass yourself off as me,
don't flatter me with 'craftsman' now
when soul's alms are what I need.

11

To Ireland, sometime before journeying there

1   I send a token to my darling,
    pour my heart-love out for her;
    poor and fair and swiftspeared Ireland —
    no tilled field is lovelier.

2   This fist of verses I send westward,
    love-pledge to her gentle seed;
    my heart is split among the quatrains
    I bestow on her families.

3   The reason for my love for Ireland
    is that I have not found her like
    nor have her wandering soldiers
    discovered such a prize.

4   I did not find in all my travels
    a country like that ancient place,

this dewy, bright arena,
this sunny, pathcrossed plain.

5   There, from me in these few phrases,
my tribute to that golden isle,
honest, mist-topped, purple Ireland —
the very type of Paradise.

6   Time for me to go to see her —
too long I've been an absentee;
that singular royal fortress,
her joy and peace suffice for me.

7   There, in the song that I send westward,
is the love that stabs me through;
O tender, brightflanked coastline,
this time I will come back to you.

8   O ancient plain with youthful features
I'm far away in foreign lands,
as if for seven dead winters exiled
with rough fetters on my hands.

9   I would never again stay absent
if I returned before death came;
where noble men are peaceful leaders
on the festive plain of the Grecian Gaels.

10   I abandon all of Europe
but you, most ancient plain,
kings' most prosperous highway,
land of giving, queen of cairns.

11 I loved you for the men that ruled you
    and loved you for your poets' wit;
    for your troops, your land, your honour,
    your clergy in a yoke condemned.

12 But most of all for sake of Éamon
    heir to pure-grassed Irish land:
    hero, who was my belovèd
    fierce and fair in curling plaits.

12

To James Butler in Ireland

1 Pure kernel of my heart, my dear friend James:
   may your life be brave, be dewed with luck in all its days.
   I send to see you, to the Irish shore,
   a darling woman who wears no clothes.

James's Answer

2 My best of friends abroad and my belovèd one:
   (though 'twas clear you left me in danger and undone)
   from the land of heroes from its valleys and its plains
   I'll send you six mercenaries to serve you over there.*

3 Of my proper, oh-so-nice Miss Modestly Well-Draped
   (a gold-haired girl with a very good name,

---

*The 'woman with no clothes' (*bean nocht* = *beannacht*) that James sent to him was called 'Miss Modestly Well-draped'.

an ever-pleasing smile, serene and cheerful face;
a beauty in truth, a glory with no grief, no hate

4   for those who of wisdom drank their fill)
a report, that she surpassed all queenly Irish girls,
has spread across the swelling swift-waved seas
along the scattered roads of Europe, to all men's ears.

5   Stamped with purity, the flower of her fair face
grew on a branch of a strong and genial race;
and saffron is not saffron when compared
with the proud amber of her plaited hair.

6   The birds that guard her head tried at Easter time
to fly, to sing their music like all their kind
till the hand of the Son of God ensnared the flock
in nets of liquid gold, expertly interlocked.

7   A more than ample forehead was discerned
between the border of her hanging curls
and her autumn-berry eyebrow; of her fine
coiffured thick yellow hair, no rib's awry.

8   Even with the warmest, coldest clouds applied
to those most precious stones, her hypnotising eyes,
there is for them no loosening or let-off
from their eternal covering of frost.

9   Without moving a hand, white and rose contest
the fiercest combat (to prove which one is best);
like torches in her cheeks they manage as a rule
to turn quickly to bright day the black-clouded noon.

10 Finer than any poet's verse is her perfect nose;
speech from her clever lips can calm alone
all sad and fearful yearning cries —
and I speak of no fairy chanting lullabies.

11 The red of her kiss-sweet delicate mouth conceals
a white-as-lily ring of finest teeth;
since Solomon's time unsurpassed's her throat
which downgrades the goose's white to coal.

12 Small perfect breasts white as foam at a ford
that hardly rise an inch, being barely grown;
hands that with fragile nimble fingers sped
making vivid samplers live in thread.

13 The many loving tribes of this proud land
that the pure and virtuous virgin banned
and sent away from life to death's strand —
who cannot go with them, his case is hard.

14 And it's a great puzzling wonder that anyone's alive
who on her, from a distance, has cast an eye,
since crowds are sick from love of her — it's no lie —
that have merely heard her face described!

13

*From Morlaix to Ireland, hearing of her oppression
under Stafford, 1632*

My protracted visit to this place overseas
leaving the land I love, her perfect, gentle peaks

and the company of those who were friends indeed:
my education's bought at this great cost to me.

The sparks that light my hearth for my native place
are her openhanded chiefs who do not forsake the faith,
her artists, her musicians, her dedicated men,
her fairhaired women whose like has not been seen.

And I hear that my belovèd is tied up in chains
with small chance of a peace-pact ever being made;
alas, oh God, to calm her trouble I can lend no hand
nor heal her open wounds, as my destiny demands.

14

In France, after dreaming

When I'm awake I am in France;
asleep, I'm in my native land.
I love my vigils less and less —
yet sleep feeds my wakefulness.

15

To my friend, from France to Ireland

Much I envy my own will
since I went ocean-travelling:
from her desire she never goes
while I'm the butt of foreign jokes;

she in royal Ireland stays,
I, in France of the crooked ways;
she is in her land at peace
and I among foreign phalanges.

When I left the Irish shore
my will's will was to stay at home,
another man, to her most dear,
received her love instead of me.

Left way behind me ever since
his side she never quits;
from her hero, curly-haired
a look she never throws my way.

My ardent will, she was beguiled
by the leader of Dunboyne —
Éamon of the curling hair
beloved, noblefeatured, brave.

Clearly in his fighter's face
appear the traits of every sage;
the pattern of the brave is here,
skill and generosity.

Music-lover, stallion-rider,
pays for poems: bless his kindness!
bestowing tunics, gold and rings
and drink at endless feastings;

keeps his promise, bloodies blades,
the small carved harp his hand has made;
to the hilt he thrusts his spear,
poets' and orphans' provisioner.

He maintains his country's fame
splendid in his native place,
slim hero of this ancient land,
lover of our Irish arts.

A new Cúchulainn, Munster's hound,
victorious in every bout:
territorial watchdog he,
licked bear of total bravery.

To that white bird, from Brittany
a blessing on Ireland comes from me:
he should not shrink from my poor prayer
packed as it is with loving grace.

Sitting or standing, uneasy till
I go home to visit him:
even to have him here would please me
so very great is my need to see him.

16

*From France to Ireland: to the same man's foot
   the time he broke it*

From withering, fine foot, keep safe —
a withering heard of far away;
many Irish palms did blaze and sting
because, O foot, of this withering.

It is good you do not ask of me
to tone my lamentation down,
for my tears are involuntary,
they are not painful but devout.

There's no misfortune — say it yet —
that could be worse than your death;
but short of that, of all ill-luck
this is the worst that could occur.

Éamon's foot in horsemanship
was no laggard, early mornings;
'och' and 'och' today is flung
that he can't change houses every month.

The administering of law abates,
diminished in control and sway,
now that my leader does not set
on Dublin's ground his footstep.

The hunting-bands of handsome Munster
grow less on the track of the deer
and the Comeraghs once heavily manned
are under the weight of a wild grief.

I promise you, great Munster,
to whom the prince was favourite son
that my knees will find no repose
until your darling's hale and whole.

17

After breaking my own foot in France

O little restless foot, suffer, in a splint encased,
since your condition's close now to my loved one's state;
in the heel of the hunt I wouldn't be much of a pal
if I didn't break my little hoof as well!

18

To Eoghan Ó Eachach after his playing a welcome
   to a certain someone

My greetings to Eoghan Ó Eachach
who, his flowing strains pursuing
the speed of his long fingers,
commands precise and gentle music.

To his girth and goodness, greetings,
and more power to his elbow;
to his strength in all its promise,
to his nicety of features.

To his wedded wife, my greetings;
her gentle man of talent,
though not in years advanced yet,
is most advanced in gracious valour.

Great anger, quick forgiveness
has the tough and shapely shining soldier,

envied by a host not churlish;
noble vessel of the skillful poets.

Comes the wind deserting venom
and the waterbird beside him
and those mad from ugly wounding,
to hear his sweet and lasting music.

The triumph of this youth in contests
carries off with his performance
the palm from every province;
impossible to hate his playing!

All peaceful people love his music,
every host, his deeds and doings;
from all foes God give him shelter
safe from evils by your marvels;

Face more fair than is a swan's face,
that in a cause was never biased,
never crooked in reckless contests;
an incense branch to rival Naoise.

Eoghan's name guides every wise man,
his name is known to all the clergy;
he has the name of education,
his name is known by all the nation.

In valour's ranks a noble lion
is my own sharp-witted Eoghan;
right, with poets in the alehouse,
to give the harp to the expert player.

In all my days, of all the men known to me,
for debating, for knowledge, for melody,
for playing arrangements in proper time,
I proclaim that Eoghan wins the prize.

19

*Airnéis**

Airnéis in English plus a diminutive,
in the excellent way our Gaelic language has,
your surpassing qualities weary me, wither me:
I am for a long time fettered by love for you.

Since first I looked on you, true pure angelic one —
that sad day you wounded me, downed me, disfigured me —
do I belong to the dead or humanity?
Is it death, this malady, or a phantom that injures me?

Never was found in the Dé Danann's poetry
one single monster who was such a shape-changer:
my state outrivals even tales told by Manannán
and he in Críoch Uisnigh incanting raised blemishes!

One day prosperous, lively, militant,
in our standing army, a mighty champion,
and if the greatest warrior in battle were my enemy
how quickly he'd die — in my imaginings!

---

*See Preface, page 11.

21

To the same

If it's a remedy for hell to be noble, loving, kind,
generous and patient in giving alms and tithes,
Tadhg and the charitable Cáit, his spouse,
will both go to Heaven's high bright house.

A fine and stately woman of lovely gentle hands
is bedmate to Tadhg and is judged to be his match;
for what they give me daily by their kind accustomed acts
they will deserve my blessing and God's thanks.

22

To Roiberd Óg Carrún

I call warm blessings on your head always
and, beloved, on the sociable pure harp you play:
with a stream of polished playing skilled and sweet
you have banished the spiders out of all our ears!

23

To Roiberd's sister

Eiléan Carrún has a polished, limpid skill:
I got a strange notion — to try surpassing it.

But after fifteen nights I'm still marvelling
at the melancholic, warm, glissando of her strings.

24

To Alison Boyton

As if they were spears that transfix, I am beguiled, alas,
by her quiet talk, her longing looks, her wonderful white face;
her blonde bundled twisted curls, her neatly coiffured hair:
that poems are made for her, Alison's unaware.

A fool the man who left a small young bride
once he had taken her to be his wife.
Why didn't he spend a week with her before he started to
    roam —
or make it a month, like we do at home?

25

To one who married on May Day

Friend and kernel of my heart: because you tie the knot
with the tribe from whom we milk the heartjuice of our love,
I am not sorry for your May Day walk
since in the dew-snail's workings you sought out your lot.

26

To Éamon Albanach

If there's anyone alive who could cause me to defect,
Éamon, with your music and your intellect,
I openly admit that you're that very man —
and after all the vows I've made my native land!

O most gentle comrade with whom I could not come
into the protective company of that wise and friendly man;
give me totally to Éamon, if it's me he wants —
don't offer me to anyone who comes from Ireland.

27

What is this flock of young girls that I see?
Judging by the actions and the speech
of this cool-palmed multitude,
you'd think them children of a king and queen.

They always act with perfect sense,
their pace is slow although the road is smooth;
the prudence of these ladies is no lie:
I hail the staid respectable young group.

There was in every girl's face
(my sudden love for them will last)
red blood infused through lime-white cheeks
applied by a friendly Expert's hand.

One couldn't but pass judgements on their traits
which suffered from no faults at all;
I heard no laughter, no voice raised
that to any would cause shame.

Each noble love, each lovely limb,
each bare knee, each pointed shoe,
each bright flank, those white neat teeth:
this muster of young daughters I salute.

My attitude to them can be believed;
to give them all my heart is right —
my best, beyond my all-embracing love,
to the daughters of the daughter of O Brien.

28

To the slanderer

Oh you who censure me for my poetic style
what is my work to you, whether weak or fine?
If it contains a foolish fault or a careless rhyme
is there any danger that you must pay the price?

Ignore, or wink, at every lapse you find
and I will treat your sins in kind;
when peaceful, yes, I'm apt to be quite mild
but when angry you had best not trust my bite.

I'd say 'twas envy gave your talk some force,
and if the same disorder through me coursed,

an old-style script perhaps for you I'd weave
whose language would be sharp as sharp could be.

From all the foolishness my pen sets down
for my Éamon, king in his own territory,
if he alone got from it fun or glee
and all the rest reviled it, 'twould be no loss to me.

29

Dirge on the death of Éamon Mac Piarais Buitléir, 1640

1   Stand aside you band of keeners,
you've said your fervent verses of bereavement;
leave the tomb of this true leader
to me a while, to recite my grief-song.

2   It is my right to complete his burial,
it is my right to make known his story;
right for me his career to speak of
since I best know his glorious doings;

3   From his childhood hard in striving
— though a soldier, he was friendly —
to his death so much lamented
I will look closely at his actions.

4   I'll not recount the tribes I'm seed of,
not alliances of my people,
nor long lines of hoary numbers
of the pedigree of this leader;

5   I'll not recount his love so pleasing,
    though I saw in public in his features
    his constant longing and devotion,
    his confidence in me and his affection.

6   Though I had the best from this regal person
    of horses, jewels, riches,
    though he did not lord it over my lowness
    or even ever leave me quiltless,

7   it's when I count his superb knowledge —
    though his charm was clear as sunlight —
    I touch upon his truest mettle,
    the stately sun-room of his disposition:

8   since I have known that griffin's wisdom,
    his manners that excelled all other's,
    'twould be a sin of grave omission
    for me, above all, not to lament him.

9   O people who pity all wretches in bondage,
    here is a wretchedness, quite unparalleled,
    here, the reckless discordant sorrow;
    here, the grief, the most grievious hardship!

10 Gormfhlaith could not match my grieving
    if she left Niall's tomb and she stood beside me;
    nor Deirdre with harsh and poignant sighing
    in isolation crying for Naoise;

11 nor beautiful Oisín the spear-man
    after sweet-voiced Fionn O Baoisgne,
    nor the wife of Hector, son of Priam,
    for the death of that shield of the Trojans.

12 It was no wonder that I'd broadcast
    the widespread yearning of the people;
    I, among the high and lowly,
    who had, of all, most cause for mourning.

13 His death's caused grief in all the country
    of Con, of Flan, of Corc, of Críomhtann,
    caused every group to bow in sorrow   .
    to the depths of low anxiety;

14 caused in lakes an overflowing,
    made great stars fierce that once were joyous,
    put jet-black drapes on all the heavens,
    made planets in the sky look cruel,

15 his death's made storms come out of calmness,
    has quenched the moon and stars at night-time,
    has dried up waves, has dried up fountains,
    has caused no sun to shine at noonday;

16 caused tumult in the rattling wind-cry,
    has caused lightning to flick through it
    like an accomplice — fiery magic —
    and fused the elements together.

17 No salmon stayed in the pleasant rivers,
    no tree-top in the wood but withered;
    the mountains wore a wet frieze tunic,
    a fine black fog was on every hillock.

18 The rain bears witness to his dying
    and grass and flowers that die in forests,
    the milk that flows to a dying trickle:
    his death fulfills all these conditions.

19 My lament will get supported
   by a hundred other lamentations
   and Nature will not grant excuses
   if I hide one teardrop for my hero:

20 for there came a rush of instant grieving
   from poets, princes, and from leaders;
   the strong, the weak, the fool, the wise man,
   the wretch, the sickly and the orphan:

21 their anxiety is no wonder
   since the loss is shared among them;
   they lost a chief, a royal one chosen —
   clerics their father, art its patron,

22 the poor its cow, the vagrant shelter,
   the widow her steadfast tree of concord,
   women their sweetheart and their lover,
   the peasants their head, their heart, their promise.

23 This ruin of all, it digs its way through
   every humane and upright nature;
   severe chastising, this death of Éamon
   who did not return from combat.

24 Though he styled himself as baron,
   this fine man was better than earls are;
   lord of Dunboyne, loved by ladies,
   judge of thousands in Tipperary.

25 Pearl, among Éamons of his wineblood,
   brave precious stone among the chieftains,
   precious gem of the lions who made him,
   beloved ridge-pole of his soldiers;

26 aggressive in authority over fighters
    as a warring-band's commander,
    flower of fierce flying columns,
    whelp of the vigorous Butler bloodline.

27 An Aodh Eangach to whom poets were constant,
    a new Guaire, swift with payments;
    the stag of his day, most ready with riches,
    hawk of the routs, the arts, the sages,

28 hero of stallions who never rested,
    hero of swift well-made war-horses,
    hero of hunting-dogs, harps and music,
    energetic and hound-surrounded;

29 head of the hunt on stony hill-slopes
    driving deer out of deepest hiding,
    head of champions not defeated,
    head of the cantering prancing cavalry.

30 Where shall I find a voice so polished
    as to praise our great wine-giver
    and to praise him over others
    but in the choice words of the scholars?

31 All I can do is omit the pedigrees
    and press ahead, praising my soldier;
    of him nothing can be recounted
    if the truth were told, but fame — a prince's.

32 In this prince there was no boasting;
    no arrogance, no vice, but virtue,
    generous, manly, showing true mercy;
    pleasant and of miraculous dignity.

33 And in my ruler, gentle, ardent,
   was a ready openhandedness —
   a giver, with comeliness and prowess,
   a noble doer of dangerous actions;

34 scanner of pedigrees, wit and wise man,
   strong fighter, pain-endurer,
   stone-caster, spear-thrower,
   griffin-like militant in valour.

35 He was tender with gentle people,
   he was firm and pressed his enemies;
   he was noble with the nobles
   and was humble among the humble.

36 He was giving, grave and well-escorted,
   he was genial, loving, thoughtful;
   he was lively, brave and wily,
   he was fierce and angry in encounters.

37 He was for scouting, schools and stallions,
   he was to clergy kindly, kingly,
   he was for hounds; supportive, landed,
   prodigal, spendthrift, openhanded.

38 In his person, athletic among warriors,
   he was mighty, lovely, whiteskinned;
   he was persistent, swift in conflict,
   he was, in arms, a venomous serpent.

39 He was mindful, devout and genial,
   he was godly, loyal, pure-minded;
   in the vigour of his wisdom, perfect,
   though in career and age a youngster.

40 Happy weaving complex verses,
   polished, eloquent, intelligent,
   musical, sociable, wisemen's crony;
   he had walls and towers and townlands,

41 he had camps and herds of livestock;
   he was strong among his soldiers,
   with worklike crowds, convivial, treating,
   entitled to the rents of territories.

42 Och my ruin, this final ruining —
   ruin of clergy and the destitute,
   ruin of wretches, laymen, lenders,
   ruin of satirists, poets, scholars.

43 There is not one alive in Ireland
   (unless he's totally benighted)
   who ever looked on his mild features
   who did not pour out longing love for him;

44 and Éamon never saw companions,
   intimate, alien, guest invited,
   to whom he would not give affection —
   even if it were an enemy;

45 but let this stand, without forgetting:
   though it was more than once I witnessed
   strong foes aiming at his ruin,
   it was he who won the victories.

46 And you elegant band of mourners
   do not consider with amazement
   what made agreements serene and peaceful
   between comely Éamon and crowds of people:

47 a most learned reader of old writings
   says no quality or condition
   is better than straightforward kindness
   for getting affection from the people:

48 this is what he said, if truthful.
   There was no man, since came the Deluge,
   to whom loyal love was more proper
   than this warrior I weep for;

49 who possessed in his heart's chambers
   in basic forms, in their quintessence,
   kindness, goodness, generosity,
   hospitality never bettered.

50 Eccentric Guaire did not proffer
   (nor that young man whose eye was offered)
   more than was given by my hero —
   and note their amplitude and fortune.

51 Nothing could stop his gifts arriving
   but the shame of poets at their value,
   their embarrassment and their silence
   at getting payments for every poem.

52 Like a sea his hand with riches,
   a regal flood-tide its bestowing,
   and it poured out without ebbing;
   a never-subsiding tide of ocean.

53 He gave cattle, steeds with saddles,
   jewels of all kinds, silk and satin,
   every armour fit for valour:
   swords and spears, shields and helmets.

54   And he gave in equal measure
gold and silver, scattered for spending:
both of them uncounterfeited,
secretly minted in his mansions.

55   And I say true, with vows as witness,
there is no nook of our Irish garden
where the destitute, the beggar,
did not benefit from his royalty.

56   His bright, delightful fortress-mansion,
(Cill Teimhnéin of the outcast scholars)
home of young girls and of clergy,
home of clans, both Irish and Normans;

57   home of heroic venomous soldiers,
home of families, of maids, of virgins,
home of mild and modest females,
home of chiefs, to which all roads led;

58   mansion full with foods and peoples,
of the liveliest drinking-parties,
of many varied wines and feastings,
never, never, mean with spices;

59   and of musical melodious settings,
gentle dexterous fingering
in harmonious clear phrasing,
to the best of classic metres.

60   If noble Jason lived in these times
he would not send his fleet to Colchis
to seek out, with great disaster,
a golden fleece surpassing sheeps' fleece,

61   had he been warned that on some human
      a fleece of purest gold would flourish
      such as grew, combed out and piled-up,
      on the head of my bright hero.

62   The sun, departing west and setting
      in pleasant, calm and lovely weather,
      is an image of his face most cherished
      and the smiling welcome through it.

63   A forehead broad with manly eyebrows,
      brilliant eyes like precious gemstones,
      mouth and cheek like glowing embers,
      a nose which mocked all snub-noses;

64   slender neck, breast bright and flaxen,
      fairest waistline, broadest shoulders,
      strong arms, with each hand perfect,
      and fine calves, capable and hose-clad.

65   Noble hound from kings descended,
      of clamorous merry Munster,
      of pleasant-rivered Leinster,
      of lavish-mansioned Ulster;

66   Norman blood from royal households —
      of the true vine, lasting offshoots:
      their best the source of all his breeding —
      he has their flower, their chief trophy:

67   blood of leaders, Tál and Cárthach,
      Mac Oilill blood, a griffin's lineage;
      blood of Eireamhón, son of Míleadh,
      blood of Rógh and of Íth the Golden;

68 blood of Burkes not crushed by foemen,
    blood of Barrys who burned their warship,
    blood of Roches of the conquering warbands,
    all in his blood, gushing vigorously.

69 His own nobility would stretch in quantity
    beyond whatever was demanded
    back through every generation
    however ignoble his forefathers.

70 Great the obedience of his levies,
    blue-eyed husband of the Siúir,
    husband of the gentle Feóir,
    lover of Shannon and net-filled Liffey.

71 A man just right as the regions back-up,
    protecting them with his fists' shadow;
    earls have long paid taxes to him
    and in his court have answered charges;

72 and to his steward, humbly, lowly,
    would bend the knee of every viscount;
    and spur and blade and polished lances
    were signs of tribute to my hero.

73 Lords to him gave military service
    when he demanded dues from nobles;
    there was a troop beneath his stirrup
    who were mighty in state and boldness.

74 And I do not count as a boastful reckoning
    (though a flock of them paid him taxes)
    his opinion of barons or viscounts
    who had earls in his service:

75 Kildare's earl, oak-like to foemen,
    Thomond in Munster of the militia;
    that Earl who was in Meath to westward
    and Earl Fingall, who led their company.

76 He took no submission that was not owed him —
    even if he took more than I'm relating —
    that Manannán of the Youth of Munster,
    Phoenix of fighters, their true flower.

77 He is a great loss to the people,
    many today are poor and naked;
    his like's not found except in visions
    by Irish people dreaming of him.

78 Great is the tearful woe for Éamon
    in the mind of woman, poet, retainer:
    palms ablaze and gravestones polished
    and tears of blood poured in a deluge.

79 'Uch!' aloud's my lasting duty:
    but I'll have ready to reproach me
    floods of 'uch' and 'uch' said lowly
    for my ever-loyal darling.

30

*Dialogue between Muircheartach Ó hIfearnáin
and the yellow cloak*

Muircheartach:
'Ease to your hurt, O yellow mantle:

your ripping causes great sadness;
although your colour makes cold cover,
your tearing is no cause for laughter.

It hardly matters, old companion,
if a fence-post caused the ripping,
or after showers if you're discarded —
you're already a disfigured cripple.

If on a peg I was to put you,
though you're threadbare, you'd be blushing;
inside you're rough, outside no better —
you're definitely for the bushes.

Not desire for gold or silver
caused you three times to be altered:
not to save your rain-stained body —
but because I am a pauper.

I have you with me far too long now,
ten half-years — and you're still with me;
your worn nap can't patch a garment,
I can't trust your ancient stitches.

You have lost your pile these ages,
you fall in bits from off my shoulders;
for my head you are no helmet,
no shelter to my back from coldness.

Time for me to stop this wrangling
and stick you on a bush, companion:
you tawny cripple with no middle;
and as for shelter, alas, I'll have none.'

The Cloak:
'Unjust, to throw me on the bushes,
you who wore at first my hem out;
you were well done-by while I lasted:
now I'm holed and old and flimsy.

I was your suit and your bedclothing
on cold nights of total blizzards;
around your head and feet a cover —
the best sweetheart you ever lived with.

And, oh my friend, if thus you reason
"bitter old things, bright are new ones",
that I'm now worn out and blemished
is the evil end of a bad union.

'Tis equal to a man past caring
whether he is high or humble
but woe to him who thus has left me
for a frieze of oil and butter.'

Muircheartach:
'Even though you're smooth, you're threadbare,
and I pity your thin framework:
there's worse disgrace in this merciless era —
you know our nobles are disabled.'

The Cloak:
'That gang of the snug and downy mantles?
I'm much easier to manage;
although I'm old and soaking
I can be dried out much faster!'

Muircheartach:
'You're a wretch and feebleminded!
You're wrinkled, you defy resewing!
Though the threads in your side show clearly
that's no excuse for your ignoring!'

31

After the beginning of this war in Ireland, 1641

Rise up my country with God's aid:
be roused up by the Son of Mary;
may an angel, above the land,
protect your high places.

It's time for the wife of Art
to quickly change her situation —
away from the destructive rain
that pours on her without cessation.

Because so long is Banbha's land
yoked by cruel desperation,
in the very mouth of brute force
under clouds of tribulation

there's no demeaning mutilation,
outright wrong or deep insulting,
no suffering in her subjection
that she has not put up with.

Though then it was not thought of,
now, from too much harshness

and because her ways were braver,
Ireland kicked in her spancel.

And God knew his land:
he looked with eyes of mercy
on the danger to the church
and to Ireland's noble persons,

of whom were still kept alive,
of the seed of that old nation,
totally resolute young men,
sparks of defence and preservation,

who will bring to pass
the revival of Gaelic glory
after long injustice to their tribes,
as their prophets forecast;

now that suddenly there has come
to the island of the Irish
that which all her patrons and her saints —
the cream of her pure people — promised:

and the reason why the cavalry of Fál
have begun to muster
is to protect our clergymen,
and not from pride and bluster;

and because some gangs have pushed
to the heights of harm-doing,
brimming with stark hate,
crimes aimed at our clergy;

till Ulstermen wildly blazed —
and the Leinster heroes —
into a multiform crimson spark,
into a lesson for the people.

Now, since the land has risen,
each man should do his damnedest
to keep his property — and head —
from being taken by this rabble.

All the men of Ireland,
each tribe, each individual,
in the dappled land of high smooth peaks
must fight for her or fall,

for if they come here again,
that terrible gang of aliens
with their soundest, choicest troops,
Éire no longer will be Éire.

So let all the men,
soldiers of this fortress island,
who're not grave-sick in burial-grounds,
turn their utmost care to Ireland;

they fear no enemy now:
for it is already manifest
that God's hand is in the fight
though he built this phantom barrier.

Now or never seems the time
for the chieftains of the Irish nation
to have exalted or cut down
their fame, their faith, their reputation.

Unless at once a stand is made,
let heavy blame on me be planted,
they may never get the chance again
although our prophet once did chant it.

God be with them; still their enemies;
it is their right after such anxiety:
the progress of this threatening deluge
is right good reason for bellicosity.

Since the Gael's apostle promised
that there never, never would be
an eclipsing of their faith
all over our ancient country,

and since he procured for his own clan
a period long and peaceful,
from oppression in this war
let Pádraig protect his people.

Their lack of weapons is made up for
by the spirit of the army,
by the war-zeal of its champions,
supported by their deeds of valour.

Making peace in concord,
submitting to their leaders' wisdom —
that is how they'll conquer hardship
and win, through slaughter, conflicts.

If the Irish soldiers keep to
rights and wages granted, be obedient,
they will not be allowed to suffer;
the law of God being in agreement.

Rise up, Ireland, with the God of Grace!
May her banner of the holy cross protect her race!
May legions of God's angels watch over, as before,
her strong levied armies in the war!

May the edge of the sharp spears by hate honed,
wielded by our chivalry — our youths as their support —
deal deadly blows, piercing to the bone,
slashing and tearing, annihilate the foe!

32

To Mathghamhain Ó hIfearnáin

This prince, the chosen of the summer fields,
this year-old calf* — so noticed is its loss
when counting cattle on the plain of Aodh —
means more to me than any herd or flock.

Though eager, tender, nimble, eloquent, in tune
with its strange, harmonious, lonesome, thought-
   provoking tone,
flute-like, searching, husky, noisy, sweet,
this calf's disturbing music causes me to sleep.

---

*Pun on 'gamhan' element in the name Mathghamhain.

33

To the Bishop on the day of his consecration

Young man, who at the right time, stole the love of all the
    priests,
by your accumulated virtues, your talents and good deeds —
since Christ's bestowed a chair befitting your career,
may you live to wear the mitre for many long years.

34

*On his being held by foreigners, with his captain,
    Lieutenant Mac an tSeannaigh, 1646*

A pity that I cannot share captivity with those
who came back from battling with the crack-troops of our
    foes,
and the grief and ill-deeds done them by the aliens
(unless the Lord unfetter these righteous men).

Even if surrounded by companions after this,
the intellectual conversations of poets and of priests,
given cows by every chieftain, every luxury,
I know that I'd be lonely with them not here.

35

*After the making known of their treachery and their
fratricide, in making peace with heretics, and after the
crowd known as the Faction raised its head, i.e., selfish
people who, in treachery and oath-breaking, cut
themselves off from the Catholic body known as the
Confederation, i.e. from the alliance of peace and assis-
tance and covenant which Irish people made among
themselves under Bible oaths re making war and
protecting the true faith in Ireland.*

1   Rouse up your courage, my Ireland!
    Now confront your evil fate;
    do not lose heart, my country,
    at your treacherously neglected state.

2   Betrayal was practised as surely
    as ever a land was betrayed:
    the finesse of the slash at your windpipe
    surpassing the enemies' usual ways.

3   And all the more ugly the horror
    done by the Irish on Irish men:
    the chieftains to whom all paid taxes
    using treachery on their own.

4   Ireland gave to these people
    the right to rule foreign tribes
    and although the strongest were chosen
    the strongest were not the best choice —

5   for it's they who ruin their mother —
    pitiless sons in a stoney place —

ignoble sick-house excrement,
these poisonous snakes in her breast;

6   who cheated her, not pitied —
no greater guilt, perhaps —
who sold church, land and sanctuary:
their hate's no momentary lapse;

7   under guise of peace sought conflict,
reneged upon their precious faith;
botched a treaty — after swearing:
to exalt them is a thing you'd hate.

8   The tribe of Israel once in Egypt
under oppression by God's foes,
under dark and magic hexes —
(a nice example for our fold)

9   after coming through the Red Sea safely,
a way impossible before —
around them waves like mountains,
their footprints on the bright sea floor,

10   a way which drowned strong armies
pursued by the rough sea's foam:
no weapon broke, no soldiers clashed,
in that famous flood of silent blows.

11   The Lord continued miracles,
the sky rained down in heavy showers
the finest-tasting, freshest rations:
their satiety in heavenly flour.

12 Every taste the young men wanted
was in the manna, so each thought:
the droves of people got a share of
the instant banquet of the Lord;

13 without hardship, ploughing, working,
and to feed so large a crowd —
until now this desert people
had no more than one day's food.

14 Until, loathing this dew of heaven,
the mean and poor among God's tribe
said it was gall, this rain celestial,
and from their grumbling broke loose pride.

15 'Alas, that we don't have from Egypt
all her roots and all her herbs,'
(acrid onions, nasty garlic!)
'here our lack of them is hard'.

16 So said these senseless wretches
till God maimed this tribe of brass
with death and great distress:
for him a loyal tribe's more apt.

17 The tribe of Israel — that is Ireland;
Egypt is her captive state;
her Red Sea and miracles
the beating of a foreign élite.

18 Her flour down from Heaven
is God's church with its own light;
flawless, flowing, abundant nurture,
rich in the Body of Christ.

19   Their ease without hardship is the succour
       that pours divinely on Ireland's head;
       land and sea, God and people:
       which of these will not come as a flood?

20   Egypt's herbs and succulent tubers —
       the crooked ways of the perverse faith,
       schemes hatched out in darkness,
       the worst of the law and rules of its reign.

21   The Hebrews' yearning for the weeds of Egypt —
       the desire of the Confederates
       for foul weeds of a fleshly credo:
       to step from the right path is to fail.

22   That same desire's among our young men,
       the great danger is still there:
       there's fear that they who first were turncoats
       have not left this place.

23   Great shame, in the name of justice,
       for a race quite naturally astute,
       to have 'reasons of state' steering their vessels
       instead of a rule that forbade them to loot;

24   that excessive desire for the church's chattels,
       which once made them excommunicate,
       will bring a blush to the cheeks of their children
       who will inherit in future days.

25   Woe to him who'd cause the world's contempt to
       fall on the land of our beginnings,
       when what was always due to its children
       was fame for deeds by generous kings.

26 To have the name of liar, apostate,
    after the talk has spread abroad,
    being applied to the land as a catchphrase
    of sorrow's kindling is the cause.

27 Should not the foremost Norman-Irish
    be vexed by this fresh slur?
    Once, for insulting the dew of heaven
    the deaths of many Jews occurred.

28 No one knows what end is destined
    for those who defame the blessed God;
    though the fact's worse than the symbol,
    salvation's nearer than the rod.

29 Luther's friends reject John Calvin
    (and rightly so — his poison does pervade):
    you see how the one opposes the other —
    and here before you is our lovely faith!

30 The faith of Christ, the faith of Luther
    (a warrior in Beelzebub's force):
    to combine them again to serve the system
    is like folding embers in snow.

31 Christ is witness to the folly
    of this small world's wisdom and its law:
    he who moves with every weather
    is he who aims at strife and war.

32 Look to yourself, oh land of Ireland:
    consider the might of those who fell;
    don't miscalculate the number
    of those on whom you can depend.

33 Of that tribe who through spite became crooked
in religion's and loyalty's cause
reject until the brink of doomsday
every feeble family's spawn.

34 Because of their descent from Míleadh
honour is not theirs alone:
ask if Inchiquin and Thomond
stay faithful to their own.

35 Oh, action wins — not talk, not charters
of the Confederation's plans:
with 'defend the faith' as pretext
it's all the worse for Ireland.

36 An evil spark, not live nor lasting,
is he who will not join the good
for the sake of friendship and alliance
but clings to ties of flesh and blood.

37 Just is the cause of all those soldiers
who, more than others, suffered pain
for the faith with zeal and gusto
and did not prevaricate.

38 Here's a clan that's a clan in earnest!
To them should be offered the juice of your breasts;
although in rank they were the lowest
they are the loyalest.

39 Not they who ask for place or honours,
nor to destroy a man's success —
your land, by right, theirs without envy,
your rent theirs to possess.

40   One thousand six hundred, six and forty —
     by certain count, the years since Christ —
     the time for victory for our nobles:
     I've never seen morale so high!

36

To Feidhlim Ruadh Ó Néill

1   All his great tribe — it's thought he surpasses them
     because of wild exploits at Áth done especially:
     Feidhlim Ó Néill the choice of all royalty —
     what better theme for poets writing currently?

2   Of the armoured Clan Tuathail this strictest of
       taskmasters,
     hater of aliens, despoiler of foreigners,
     Feidhlim Ó Néill whose work is protecting us
     safeguard our love for our famous warriors.

3   If people are asked about Feidhlim the nobleman,
     they say guarding our land should be left to him
     as his spear has been washed in unceasing hostilities —
     though 'twould be more right if he acted as peacemaker.

4   It's proven by him with a true patron's utterance
     that he is a prop to protect all the virtuous;
     he holds back no work nor fine precious offering
     nor his gentle bright skin from wounding or injury.

37

To Tiobóid Butler

1 I'm ageing and I feel I've been too long alive,
   too weak to travel, pouring out my cries;
   no cash, no grain, no horse — no, not a thing put by —
   and those whom my trouble would pain, they do not
   survive.

2 The Anamhan's high lord is the cause of all my grief:
   to live without him is not living, for me;
   alas that I did not die in his day —
   his talk was loving and intimate.

3 I lost him and I never shall see again his kind,
   the lavish man who leaves Solohead behind;
   prompt to pay for poems with his most precious things,
   scattering largesse into his poets' keeping.

4 The slaughter of the strong is no worse to me
   than the packing of their friends alive overseas;
   if, after years, they come from this venturing —
   I'll not live to see them, I'll not benefit.

5 No good to me that he sailed out of my ken —
   the gentlest, the kindest, the noblest of men;
   the lovely nurturer, the watchman of my life,
   a strong support to me his hand was and his voice.

6 Smiter of all robbers, of implacable pursuit,
   helper of our weak and of our destitute;
   I parted with my soul when Tiobóid went away,
   long, long to me seems to pass a week or day.

7 Alas, that I did not become a gaunt vagabond
   (may no sorrow come to me because I love this man)
   so that wherever he would be, whatever land or shore,
   I'd be there, reciting for him my poems.

38

1 My sad day, Ireland of the old high hills,
   is this latest chapter of your ills;
   your fair skin torn by the foreign herd,
   your body, bone and sinew, ripped to shreds.

2 From venomous black clouds death comes down
   and we cannot listen to the horror of the rain;
   you could not manage alert shepherding
   for wolves and outlaws crawled about your skin.

3 Plague in the air and violence let loose
   tortured your women, exhausted your troops,
   trampled up together your milk and your grain,
   the fish do not leap to the top of the cascade.

4 Kinship and love were totally denied,
   hospitality let lapse in spite of ancient rites,
   clerics of learning have become very scarce,
   and as for giving alms, no one seems to care.

5 Field of white dwellings, our ancestral field,
   your disaster brings misery to me;
   though you cried in torment for your flawless flock
   death has snatched them underground with no way back.

6 Éamon of Cill Aonaigh (I love that prince),
  spouse of poets through all his hand dispensed,
  fierce wise warrior quick to draw the blade,
  rectifying wrong on the tombstoned plain.

7 The seed of lethal fathers, of true Gaelic blood,
  and the seed of high-ranking ancestors,
  the sharp-bladed offspring of heroes of our past,
  all stopped protecting you, a most shameful act.

8 The long-surviving seed of bright forefathers fade,
  the generous and savage sons of Maev decay;
  those who sprang from vigorous strong men
  and the first foreigners' flower, their time has ebbed.

9 They, who should have come to your aid,
  have generated now all the world's hate,
  since they laid their blades aside without one stroke
  and bowed to the rotten rabble Saxon yoke.

10 They consented to banishment over the sea
  (how many went to Spain is not clear to me),
  and alas I cannot for certain write
  whether they will return to us in my lifetime.

11 Oh green-branched Ireland of most lovely shades,
  you were defiled by every passing stain;
  not one herb to relieve you grew by your side:
  for your fierce fighting-men your vigour had died.

12 There's danger we're deserted because of ugly guilt;
  O good mother Mary, our holy kin,
  get us freedom from oppression for we are weak-willed,
  as alms from the God to whom you gave your milk.

39

It shames and pierces me with pain,
this defilement of our derelict plain —
our strong warriors once known for skill and speed
unmanned are banished overseas.

Dregs of the Saxon pack, with idiot-eyes,
in their place have come to power in pride;
I, alone, in unshared danger stay,
my poems are unread, I get no pay.

40

1 It causes me vast sorrow and makes my anguish great
to see our Irish army in such a desperate state;
aliens among them destroy and decimate,
hunger is killing them and fever from the plague.

2 The tangle of their sins made God horrified:
yielding to weak ways they lost their strength and pride;
the bravest of these heroes were cornered in West Clare
and rioting Saxons came in to take their place.

3 The outlook they adopted has long caused shame —
since they rid themselves of comrades who crossed the
    waves
(they don't even know how many went to Spain!)
they laid down their arms and no battle gave.

4 They who live in our land and the carnage survive
to avoid all that is good — that's their desire —

flaying the weak, their usual prey,
in spite of whose curses they ask for no grace.

5   Without the fighters whom my poems would please,
I am become feeble and am made old by grief;
if they ever come — and hard it's to return —
I'll not be here to see them, for death will have won.

6   Of the venom and deceit many men have used
on the persons of our clergy, our leaders of repute,
and in beating on the battlefield our fighting men,
I don't know which, but one will surely win.

41

After the Irish laid down their arms

1   Oh Christ, how long and sad and bitterly I wail
lamenting for the troops of Ireland's cold plain,
to rest is not right from the terror of my pain —
a hundred heard my voice far away in Spain.

2   A swift Suibhne I, with a troubled brain,
a Caoilte beside the noble Fianna's graves;
aged beyond the norm, with a withered face,
my heart's a tangled heap of torn sad remains.

3   My madness like the madness which unhinged Deirdre
        on the day
that whitefingered flower heard Naoise was in his grave;
my howl to the hollows of the mountains reached
furrows on my face from my teeming tears.

4   When I was young, in full flower in my career,
    the calming songs of scholars were construed
        harmoniously;
    by the shoulders of tall Éamon my reward was sweet
    when my poem was woven and I received my fee.

5   My heart's weighed down with terror since the deaths
    of the kindly scholars of Cluain an Éisg,
    by whom I was honoured always with great state —
    and now we are bested and in desperate straits.

6   Alas to me the situation's clear:
    our loss of poets, our strong men in defeat;
    dangerous proclamations on our ordained priests
    come from the hatred of the fierce pack overseas.

7   Leaders of our regions, once our sheltering walls,
    by this surly rabble were banished from us all;
    they are always moving swiftly to the far-off north
    in the wind and the cold with the clouds making war.

8   By the breastwork of a harbour I went alone
    greatly lamenting the danger to our homes;
    our enemy destroys our crops, our stock is in his hands,
    and worse he sells us off like a flock of lambs —

9   an unnatural act, this disruption of a race,
    and all who sailed from our protecting plain —
    their lovely mansions' masonry, their fine white towers,
    were blown up and scattered about on the ground.

10 Oh kind nurse of the high and powerful God,
    beg boldly of the infant who is your flesh and blood,

beg of him when he has suckled at your breasts
to end the evil deeds of these foreigners.

42

To my long-loved Raymond of the ready verses,
to his fine band of freeborn friends: I forward them
a bitter souvenir of absence and affection
confined on Maldon Strand in hard imprisonment.

43

Outburst of Sorrow and Dirge for the Lieutenant-
General of Munster, i.e. Richard Butler, son of
the Viscount (Uí Chuirín)

Here, the outburst

1   Och, is it possible? Och, not possible!
    Och, were it possible to better my state!
    Gone into the ground is my beloved Richard
    and I, like one doomed, alive in his wake.

2   A man once thought another Moses,
    who rescued Ireland from her woe,
    a man bent always on relieving
    the evil fate of the Church of Rome.

3   The proven noble son of Piaras,
    a phoenix of phalanxes: taken all in all,

there was no one like him in combat when cornered,
none more loving, more wise, more jovial.

4   The young, correct, swift, slender chieftain,
the steady mast, urging on his men;
without thwarting any of equal ranking,
such was he, a great and spirited prince.

The Lament for the same man

5   Oh Richard Mac Piarais, the last of our party,
the cause of our sorrow, our bedrock of loving:
although you have died our plight has not vanished
but is crowned with more woe since your going from us.

6   While you were alive, oh lion of power,
our ancient land was boldly hopeful
of recovering from her enemies' onslaught
and the church of the return of tributes;

7   all that hope was deferred, however,
when your death occurred, oh lovely noble;
may Heaven deign to rain its graces
on our overwhelmed homeland.

8   Forgive the time I was not intoning
laments for you, who left me broken;
I gave a chance then at your tombstone
for a multitude instead to mourn you.

9   My eyes not idle for a season
have poured out floods of weeping

and terrible harsh cries prevented
my power to compose a sentence.

10   Though great for your blood's seed my love is
and greater still your love for me was,
I swear with haste, loud on the bible,
that that is not why I now describe you;

11   but because when virtue's in the balance
I do not know an old or young man —
or any man of better talent
who could compete beside you.

12   Foe or friend I defy to assert that
one of their years ever attained to
the excellence of character you came to
or your intellectual reputation.

13   Oh forsaken and exhausted Irish,
would you like to hear recited
some of the noble soothing stories
of our much-loved man of prowess,

14   which forever will be related
in every language to the learned
as examples to their youngsters,
as reproaches to their elders?

15   Although every noble blood in Ireland
was poured upon his head as birthright
he still garnered useful learning
(in his kind a trait not common).

16 Though only a little over thirty
    on the night that death came on him,
    as well as perfect arts, he'd mastered
    seven tongues and spoke them finely.

17 While still a youth, but yet quite manly,
    abroad he made no petty visits,
    but to *learn* in lands he travelled,
    seeking chivalry and getting it gradually.

18 There is no rank, from the most lowly
    to being the righthand man of leaders,
    that he did not hold, but emerged a hero
    not knowing fear, fatigue or sickness.

19 There was no rule of thrust and parry,
    no stratagem, no trick with ordnance,
    no advantage or chance in battle
    which he did not want, acquire and master.

20 From foreign lands and harsh conditions
    he brought treasure, fame and riches;
    to his calling and his name brought honour,
    renown for all his friends and people.

21 He brought a testimony — and what better
    to satisfy the King of England —
    from the powerful King of Poland,
    confirmed in the royal handwriting

22 that he had witnessed Richard's progress
    being always there beside him;
    at Smolensk in desert Russia
    saw him fighting one hot morning:

23   a day which saw, destroyed and broken,
     the amazing vast Baraban army
     from out of Tartary and Moscow,
     by Richard with his bold assaulting —

24   a horde known for their proven boldness
     which when numbered by a head-count
     (not including old or young men),
     came to sixty thousand soldiers.

25   He often fought at single combat
     (not bell-book-and-candle duels):
     no one ever surpassed my hero
     in attacking or defending.

26   In war-decisions no one touched him,
     like the wind in March his actions;
     every word of his was matchless,
     with authority to back his statements.

27   Coming to Ireland after his travels,
     he bedded many kindly women,
     noble lovers suited to his station
     from whom he got offspring of great beauty.

28   He spent time in a comfortable residence
     with a celebrated lavish household,
     and throughout Ireland he was famous
     for the intense humanity he radiated;

29   with no surliness, with no door-shutting,
     crowds were received in his bright mansion,
     served most kindly with true welcome —
     every guest, whether noble or humble.

30　At the start of this war for St Patrick's people,
　　for the faith that has no falsehood,
　　Richard rose with a papal knighthood
　　at the head of brave strong levies,

31　inciting, teaching, urging,
　　rousing and filling them with courage,
　　steering, uniting them for conflict —
　　a singular teacher of chivalrous legions;

32　and though the smiter lost on occasion
　　through lack of horses, arms and engines,
　　still he bore, the lovely griffin,
　　his share of valour at these moments.

33　He was before the gate at Mallow,
　　his skin in shreds from being shot at;
　　fourteen holes in his clothes were counted
　　from the firing of swift lead bullets.

34　At Ballinard's stream, with no reinforcements,
　　in the belly of the gap he waited proudly,
　　a pillar of justice before his enemies' venom,
　　a few small remnants shooting at him

35　long after the main body had retreated;
　　the strong battalion from the country
　　behind him, his rear was in no danger
　　until they travelled to Riascach boldly.

36　His own people he brought safely with him,
　　drawn up together in formation,
　　and he waited a week before the enemy
　　after their routing, till they turned on him.

37 They would not have bound him in Liscarroll
   had he fled to the rear of the army
   or restrained his attack till the goal was taken
   or been cowardly like the fleeing cavalry.

38 And in Coill Chruaidh in spite of danger
   all the attacking was his doing,
   on foreign clans greedy for warfare,
   until they yielded to his valour.

39 When the navy of the hated foreigners
   at New Ross attacked his vessels,
   Richard there did wreck and sink them,
   left the fleet in a heap in the harbour.

40 At Cloch Liath, so said all warriors,
   at the assaulting this great man was
   like the fierce fury of a wolf after sheep-flocks,
   the swoop of a hawk on birds in the moorland.

41 At Youghal, when the alarm was sounded,
   no means of help from friends to aid him
   with a small band in the dark of nighttime
   scattered his strong foes most boldly.

42 Since he had sworn in no trivial phrases
   the allegorical vow of Fódhla,
   not to stop the war until the clergy
   regained their taxes and authority,

43 when a crooked hand was dealt by the Council
   ploughing now a transverse furrow,
   and by the cunning clergy with smooth deception
   (made blind like moles by this same Council)

44 it was not for him, our otter of triumph:
on the spot he refused unashamedly
from the State, place and promised office,
and a knighthood they pressed upon him.

45 He did not wish to break the oaths that bound him
nor to side with the State's wrong action;
he did not lie — that was not his nature —
nor side with comrades or relations;

46 but travelling every roadway northwards
from Sliabh Cláire up to Ulster
and through Ormond to the papal legate
suffered every excess from the enemy.

47 They burned his buildings and his residence,
his stout castle with its rugged portcullis,
made a foray on his unguarded holding,
his flocks, his cattle and his jewels.

48 And they made a move most barbarous —
put his heir — a child — in fetters;
his wife, his family were homeless, exhausted,
and his people were left scattered.

49 Who were the authors of these shameful actions?
Who but the clans of lovely Ireland!
Murchadh and the Confederation
without honour betrayed their mother.

50 When Richard saw this hideous action,
he offered zealously to God in prayers
all he had suffered here while living,
for the sake of Christ's suffering Passion —

51 he was not like those excommunicated,
    military favourites, unimportant leaders
    who earned the reproach of papal curses
    for losing the Faith by disputation.

52 So much good had this son of princes
    that Paradise is for him most fitting;
    for through the fault of Pádraig's people
    their company was not worth keeping.

53 This man's death is the ruin of Ireland,
    ruin of soldiers, ruin of poets,
    ruin of abandoned weaklings,
    utter ruin of monks and brothers,

54 man who gave alms to paupers
    without caution, as I witnessed;
    unusually he kept his kindness secret:
    the poor never knew what hand it came from.

55 This devout and just almsgiver
    treated weak and strong correctly;
    no friends surpassed my friend in friendship,
    no enemy in venomous anger.

56 Like a tree, in battle sturdy,
    like Fionn for wisdom, for prowess Oscar,
    like the active griffin Gall in boldness,
    like our heroic Cú Chulainn, skillful;

57 in competition, speed, dexterity,
    heroic valour, and ability
    in hunting with cunning snares, in running,
    or in mounting horses swiftly;

58 in the handling of stately war-steads
   or in leaping across flat marshland,
   in dexterous throwing of dart and javelin —
   hard to find this man's equal.

59 Bearlike fighter, in danger warlike,
   this young man adorned with courage;
   stag of his time, bull among cattle,
   Phoenix of fighting men of Ireland.

60 He was the performer, the thief of laughter,
   the postponer of depression;
   used to cheer up morose assemblies
   with his delight in poems and jesting.

61 Every girl in women's gatherings,
   however lovely, refined or highborn,
   let her beauty shun her shyness,
   through her covert love for Richard.

62 Bealach na gCloch will boast forever
   of how my prince was loved by its princes,
   how its camp stood guard of honour,
   bestowing welcome on the hero.

63 Sweet beyond sweetness was his laughter;
   on a gentle harp in lime-white mansions
   he'd make the herons sleep in calmness,
   and wounded men think their wounds were trivial.

64 There was no Aonghus, Daolghas or Dáire
   or Manannán across salty bitter water,
   no Moses, no Midhir mac an Daghdha,
   no spirit who could outdo Richard.

65 His excellent music went beyond assessing,
and poetic assemblies will be saying
for a long time after him in Ireland
that the harp will be barren and feeble.

66 Who so young was so perfect in qualities?
How would he be if he reached maturity?
Oh Richard Mac Piarais, such pain to Patrick,
Lieutenant-General of the plains of Áine.

44

To the Bishop of Léithglann

1 I left one whom it was sad to be severed from —
Oh Lord it worsens me, this severe bewilderment;
though his wealth is diminished by many plunderings,
my being beside him would guarantee my guiltiness.

2 I myself let down my Éamon of Éamons,
pearl above pearls is his rule of his countrymen;
slight the dismay of this young Irishman
at hardships in every place where the seagull settles.

3 A fresh palm-branch, this Éamon Ó Díomasa,
this noble most casual, this friend most approachable;
chieftain of freemen, who in my opinion knows
precious love-spells and every great sophistry.

4 Darling of the arts, of sons of great ancestors,
who did not come to his see to shake like an idiot;

unjust to despise this stock for their lineage —
by the charter of swords they came to be royalty.

5 Well-shaped, humane, a foe to all greediness,
   manly and deep-voiced, averse to hilarity;
   chief flower of his stock, a man truly merciful:
   not unhandsome I think this man of importance.

45

To the Bishop's companion

Dominic O Farrell, kindler of kindliness,
calms the fierce anger of poetic gatherings,
with brilliant musicianship sends out the warriors
without heart-scalding, like the gentlest of cataracts.

46

To Ireland, 1653

On Séamus Rua bestow my heart
and to his happy wife all my devotion send;
remember I am loyal to my cousins in the north
and always faithful to my long-time friends.

Constantly and quietly advise the people
that it will not be long till we come to an agreement;
to see them, in spite of my heart's tiredness,
I think I will go on a visit to Ireland.

47

To Muircheartach Ó Briain Mac Taidhg,
son of the Earl, 1654

1   Descendant of Lorc and Blod and Brian and Cas,
     since from our sad country God allowed you pass,
     success to all your journeys and sojourns
     until you move again in power on your return.

2   For all the evil you received fighting for your native place
     you will be forever known as the O Brien *per se*;
     the result of your bribe's breaking of rules and decrees
     was their borders' deliverance from oppressions and from
        fees.

3   No lord alive has nobler blood than you,
     your bravery is not surpassed by heroic troops;
     the world has heard of the good attempt you made
     to achieve what is due in love for this ancient place.

4   A supporter of your island went abroad awhile,
     until chance and stratagem ended his exile;
     I call on the height of heaven to witness here
     that your coming in is due to his career.

48

To William Duggan, for a certain reason

Tell at first as news to his lordship this:
that I don't let them flaunt the rules in the order since

a big horse was put under the arse of each priest of them
and I, a just man, have to walk like the least of men.

And then after that tell that gathering of holy men —
if you find out that gang hope for a loan from me —
though I'm most likely to be asked to part with a harness-set,
I'd rather have it stored away till the saddle rots from
    tarnishing!

49

*On hearing that it was ordered by the Irish clergy that
a brother may not compose Gaelic poetry*

I heard of late from one easy-going, friendly,
a novel tale that came out of Ireland:
that now the clergy regard as threatening
the incisive Gaelic language —
the great joy of our urbane ancestors!
I, myself, won't engage in their arguments,
since the time has gone since I could organise
each thought that came from contemplating;
when with a sharp and dangerous intellect
I could shake a fist of magic javelins
that would not lose their cunning energies
right at these overbearing clergymen
down on their bald destructive craniums!

I will sew up my lips with plaited cross-stitching
and not speak of their niggardly pettiness,
but I denounce this pack and their censoring
and their hate, O God, for my fellow-countrymen!

Sources

Saothar Filidheachta an tAthar Pádraigín Haicéad d'Ord San Dominic, Tórna (M. H. Gill, 1916)

Pádraigín Haicéad, Pearse Beasley (*Dublin Freeman*, 18 November 1920)

An Irish Dominican Poet (*Páidraigín Haicéad 1600-1654*), Seán Ó Faoláin (*Irish Rosary*, vol XXX, 1926)

Pádraigín Haicéad, an tAthair Seán Ó Siadhail B.D.L.C.L. (*Irish Rosary*, vol XXXV, 1931)

An tAthair Pádraigín Haicéad O.P., An Br. Colmán Ó Ceoinín O.P. (*The Watchman*, vol 3 no 5 June 1937)

Filíocht Phádraigín Haicéad, Máire Ní Cheallacháin (An Clóchomhar, 1962)

Duine de na Mórfhilí, Gearóid S. Mac Eoin (*Feasta*, Marta, 1963)